AF345056

Intelligence of Elephants.

Intelligence of Elephants

Collection

Nature and Human Studies

ISBN : 978-2-38469-028-2
EAN : 9782384690282

The elephant is the largest living land animal. Though numerous forms existed in early geological times, it is represented today by two species only: the African elephant, and the Asiatic elephant.

The African elephant differs from its Asiatic cousin in several particulars. The apparent distinguishing features are the tusks that attain a much greater development and occur in both sexes, while in the Asiatic species the males alone possess them. The African elephant is at least a foot higher than the Asiatic, attaining a maximum height of eleven feet. Its ears are extremely large, covering the shoulder, and in some instances measuring three and a half feet in length by two and a half feet in width, while those of its Indian relative are comparatively small.

(C. F. Holder, *The Ivory King: A popular history of the elephant and its allies.*)

Chapter 1[1]

The intelligence of the elephant is no doubt considerable, although there is equally little doubt that it is generally exaggerated. Some of the most notorious instances of the display of remarkable sagacity by this animal are probably fabulous, or at least are not sufficiently corroborated to justify belief. Such, for instance, is the celebrated story told by Pliny with all the assurance of a '*certum est*,' and repeated by Plutarch, of the elephant, who having been beaten for not dancing properly, was afterwards found practising his steps alone in the light of the moon. Although this story cannot, in the absence of corroboration, be accepted as fact, we ought to remember, in connection

[1] G. J. Romanes, in *Animal Intelligence*.

with it, that many talking and piping birds unquestionably practise in solitude the accomplishments which they desire to learn.

Quitting, however, the enormous multitude of anecdotes, more or less doubtful, and which may or may not be true, I shall select a few well-authenticated instances of the display of elephant intelligence.

Memory.

As regards memory, several cases are on record of tamed elephants having become wild, and, on again being captured after many years, returning to all their old habits under domestication. Mr. Corse publishes in the 'Philosophical Transactions' an instance which came under his own notice. He saw an elephant, which was carrying baggage, take fright at the smell of a tiger and run off. Eighteen months afterwards this elephant was recognised by its keepers among a herd of wild companions, which had been captured and were confined in an enclosure. But when anyone approached the animal he struck out with his trunk, and seemed as fierce as any of the wild herd. An old hunter then mounted a tame elephant, went up to the feral one, seized his ear and ordered him to lie down. Immediately the force of old associations broke through all opposition, the word of command was obeyed, and the elephant while lying down gave a certain peculiar squeak which he had been known to utter in former days. The same author gives another and more interesting account of an elephant which, after having been for only two years tamed, ran wild for fifteen years, and on being then recaptured, remembered in all details the words of command. This, with several other well-authenticated facts of the same kind, shows that the elephant certainly has an exceedingly tenacious memory, rendering credible the statement of Pliny, that in their more advanced age these animals recognise men who were their drivers when young.

Emotions.

Concerning emotions, the elephant seems to be usually actuated by the most magnanimous of feelings. Even his proverbial vindictiveness appears only to be excited under a sense of remembered injustice. The universally known story of the tailor and the elephant doubtless had a foundation in fact, for there are several authentic cases on record of elephants resenting injuries in precisely the same way; and Captain Shipp personally tested the matter by giving to an elephant a sandwich of bread, butter, and cayenne pepper. He then waited for six weeks before again visiting the animal, when he went into the stable and began to fondle the elephant as he had previously been accustomed to do. For a time no resentment was shown, so that the Captain began to think that the experiment had failed; but at last, watching for an opportunity, the elephant filled his trunk with dirty water, and drenched the Captain from head to foot.

Griffiths says that at the siege of Bhurtpore, in 1805, the British army had been a long time before the city, and, owing to the hot dry winds, the ponds and tanks had dried up. There used therefore to be no little struggle for priority in procuring water at one of the large wells which still contained water:—

On one occasion two elephant-drivers, each with his elephant, the one remarkably large and strong, and the other comparatively small and weak, were at the well together;

the small elephant had been provided by his master with a bucket for the occasion, which he carried on the end of his proboscis, but the larger animal, being destitute of this necessary vessel, either spontaneously, or by the desire of his keeper, seized the bucket, and easily wrested it from his less powerful fellow-servant; the latter was too sensible of his inferiority openly to resent the insult, though it is obvious that he felt it; but great squabbling and abuse ensued between the keepers. At length the weaker animal, watching the opportunity when the other was standing with his side to the well, retired backwards a few paces in a very quiet and unsuspicious manner, and then, rushing forward with all his might, drove his head against the side of the other, and fairly pushed him into the well.

Great trouble was experienced in extricating this elephant from the well—a task which would, indeed, have been impossible but for the intelligence of the animal itself. For when a number of fascines, which had been employed by the army in conducting the siege, were thrown down the well, the elephant showed sagacity enough to arrange them with his trunk so as to construct a continuously rising platform, by which he gradually raised himself to a level with the ground.

Allied to vindictiveness for small injuries is revenge for large ones, and this is often shown in a terrible manner by wounded elephants. For instance, Sir E. Tennent writes:—

Some years ago an elephant which had been wounded by a native, near Hambangtotte, pursued the man into the town, followed him along the street, trampled him to death in the bazaar before a crowd of terrified spectators, and succeeded in making good its retreat to the jungle.

Many other cases of vindictiveness, more or less well authenticated, may be found mentioned by Broderip, Bingley, Mrs. Lee, Swainson, and Watson. This trait of emotional character seems to be more generally present in the elephant than in any other animal, except perhaps the monkey.

Another emotion strongly developed in the elephant is sympathy. Numberless examples on this head might be adduced, but one or two may suffice. Bishop Huber saw an old elephant fall down from weakness, and another elephant was brought to assist the fallen one to rise. Huber says he was much struck with the almost human expression of surprise, alarm, and sympathy manifested by the second elephant on witnessing the condition of the first. A chain was fastened round the neck and body of the sick animal, which the other was directed to pull. For a minute or two the healthy elephant pulled strongly; but on the first groan given by its distressed companion it stopped abruptly, 'turned fiercely round with a loud roar, and with trunk and fore-feet began to loosen the chain from the neck.'

Again, Sir E. Tennent says:—

The devotion and loyalty which the herd evince to their leader are very remarkable. This is more readily seen in the case of a tusker than any other, because in a herd he is generally the object of the keenest pursuit by the hunters. On such occasions the others do their utmost to protect him from danger: when driven to extremity they place their leader in the centre and crowd so eagerly in front of him that the sportsmen have to shoot a number which they might otherwise have spared. In one instance a tusker, which was badly wounded by Major Rogers, was promptly surrounded by his companions, who supported him between their shoulders, and actually succeeded in covering his retreat to the forest.

Lastly, allusion may be made to the celebrated observation of M. le Baron de Lauriston, who was at Laknaor during an epidemic which stretched a number of natives sick and dying upon the road. The Nabob riding his elephant over the road was careless whether or not the animal crushed the men and women to death, but not so the elephant, which took great pains to pick his steps among the people so as not to injure them.

The following account of emotion and sagacity is quoted from the Rev. Julius Young's Memoirs of his father, Mr. Charles Young, the actor. The animal mentioned is the one that subsequently attained such widespread notoriety at Exeter Change, not only on account of his immense size, but still more because of his cruel death:—

In July 1810, the largest elephant ever seen in England was advertised as 'just arrived.' As soon as Henry Harris, the manager of Covent Garden Theatre, heard of it, he determined, if possible, to obtain it; for it struck him that if it were to be introduced into the new pantomime of 'Harlequin Padmenaba,' which he was about to produce at great cost, it would add greatly to its attraction. Under this impression, and before the proprietor of Exeter Change had seen it, he purchased it for the sum of 900 guineas. Mrs. Henry Johnston was to ride it, and Miss Parker, the columbine, was to play up to it. Young happened to be one morning at the box-office adjoining Covent Garden Theatre, when his ears were assailed by a strange and unusual uproar within the walls. On asking one of the carpenters the cause of it, he was told 'it was something going wrong with the elephant; he could not exactly tell what.' I am not aware what the usage may be nowadays, but then, whenever a new piece had been announced for presentation on a given night, and there was but scant time for its preparation, a rehearsal would take place after the night's regular performance was over, and the audience had been dismissed. One such there had been the night before my father's curiosity had been roused. As it had been arranged that Mrs. Henry Johnston, seated in a howdah on the elephant's back, should pass over a bridge in the centre of a numerous group of followers, it was thought expedient that the unwieldy monster's tractability should be tested. On stepping up to the bridge, which was slight and temporary, the sagacious brute drew back his fore-feet and refused to budge. It is well known as a fact in natural history that the elephant, aware of his unusual bulk, will never trust its weight on any object which is unequal to its support. The stage-manager, seeing how resolutely the animal resisted every attempt made to compel or induce it to go over the bridge in question, proposed that they should stay proceedings till next day, when he might be in a better mood. It was during the repetition of the experiment that my father, having heard the extraordinary sounds, determined to go upon the stage, and see if he could ascertain the cause of them. The first sight that met his eyes kindled his indignation. There stood the high animal, with downcast eyes and flapping ears, meekly submitting to blow after blow from a sharp iron goad, which his keeper was driving ferociously into the fleshy part of his neck, at the root of the ear. The floor on which he stood was converted into a pool of blood. One of the proprietors, impatient at what he regarded as senseless obstinacy, kept urging the driver to proceed to still severer extremities, when Charles Young, who was a great lover of animals, expostulated with him, went up to the poor patient sufferer, and patted and caressed him; and when the driver was about to wield his instrument again, with even still more vigour, he caught him by the wrist as in a vice, and stayed his hand from further violence. While an angry altercation was going on between Young and the man of colour, who was the driver, Captain Hay, of the *Ashel*, who had brought over 'Chuny' in his ship, and had petted him greatly on the voyage, came in and begged to know what was the matter. Before a word of explanation could be given, the much-wronged creature spoke for himself; for, as soon as he perceived the entrance of his patron, he waddled up to him, and, with a look of gentle appeal, caught hold of his hand with his proboscis, plunged it into his bleeding wound, and then thrust it before his eyes. The gesture seemed to say, as plainly as if it had been enforced by speech, 'See how these cruel men treat Chuny. Can *you* approve of it?' The hearts of the hardest present were sensibly touched by what they saw, and among them that of the gentleman who had been so energetic in promoting its harsh treatment. It was under a far better impulse that he ran out into the street, purchased a few apples at a stall, and offered them to him. Chuny eyed him askance, took them, threw them beneath his feet, and when he had crushed them to pulp, spurned them from him. Young, who had gone into Covent Garden on the same errand as the gentleman who had preceded him, shortly after re-entered, and also held out to him some fruit, when, to the astonishment of the bystanders, the elephant ate every morsel, and after he had done so, twined his trunk with studied gentleness around Young's waist, marking by his action that, though he had resented a wrong, he did not forget a kindness.

It was in the year 1814 that Harris parted with Chuny to Cross, the proprietor of the menagerie at Exeter Change. One of the purchaser's first acts was to send Charles Young a life ticket of admission to his exhibition; and it was one of his little innocent vanities, when passing through the Strand with any friend, to drop in on Chuny, pay him a visit in his den, and show the intimate relations which existed between them. Some years after, when the elephant's theatrical career was run, and he was reduced to play the part of captive in one of the cages of Exeter Change, a thoughtless dandy one day amused himself by teasing him with the repeated offer of lettuces—a vegetable for which he was known to have an antipathy. At last he presented him with an apple, but, at the moment of his taking it, drove a large pin into his trunk, and then sprang out of big reach. The keeper seeing that the poor creature was getting angry, warned the silly fellow off, lest he should become dangerous. With a contemptuous shrug of the shoulder, he trudged off to the other end of the gallery, and there displayed his cruel ingenuity on other humbler beasts, till, after the absence of half-an-hour, he once more approached one of the cages opposite the elephant's. By this time he had forgotten his pranks with Chuny, but Chuny had not forgotten him; and as he was standing with his back towards him, he thrust his proboscis through the bars of his prison, twitched off the offender's hat, dragged it in to him, tore it to shreds, then threw it into the face of the offending gaby, consummating his revenge with a loud guffaw of exultation. All present proclaimed their approbation of this act of retributive justice, and the discomfited coxcomb had to retreat from the scene in confusion, jump into a hackney coach, and betake himself to the hatter's in quest of a new tile for his unroofed skull. The tragic end of poor Chuny must be within the recollection of many of my readers. From some cause unknown he went mad, and after poison had been tried in vain it took 152 shots, discharged by a detachment of the Guards, to despatch him.

The elephant in many respects displays strange peculiarities of emotional temperament. Thus Mr. Corse says:—'If a wild elephant happens to be separated from its young for only two or three days, though giving suck, she never after recognises or acknowledges it;' yet the young one knows its dam, and cries plaintively for her assistance.

Again, in the wild state, the spirit of exclusiveness shown by members of a herd (*i.e.* family) towards elephants of other herds is remarkable. Sir E. Tennent writes:—

If by any accident an elephant becomes hopelessly separated from his own herd, he is not permitted to attach himself to any other. He may browse in the vicinity, or frequent the same place to drink and to bathe; but the intercourse is only on a distant and conventional footing, and no familiarity or intimate association is under any circumstances permitted. To such a height is this exclusiveness carried, that even amidst the terror of an elephant corral, when an individual, detached from his own party in the *mêlée* and confusion, has been driven into the enclosure with an unbroken herd, I have seen him repulsed in every attempt to take refuge among them, and driven off by heavy blows with their trunks as often as he attempted to insinuate himself within the circle which they had formed for common security. There can be no reasonable doubt that this jealous and exclusive policy not only contributes to produce, but mainly serves to perpetuate, the class of solitary elephants which are known by the term *goondahs* in India, and which from their vicious propensities and predatory habits are called *Hora*, or *Rogues*, in Ceylon.

The emotional temper, or rather transformation of emotional psychology, which is exhibited by the Rogues here mentioned, is as extraordinary as it is notorious. From being a peaceable, sympathetic, and magnanimous animal, the elephant, when excluded from the society of its kind, becomes savage, cruel, and morose to a degree unequalled in any other animal.

The repulsive accounts of the bloodthirsty rage and wanton destructiveness of Rogues show that their actions are not due to sudden bursts of fury at the sight of man or his works, but rather to a deliberate and brooding resolve to wage war on everything, so that the animal patiently lies in wait for travellers, rushing from his ambush only when he finds that the latter are within his power. As showing the cold-blooded determination of this murderous desire, I may quote the following case, as it was communicated to Sir E. Tennent:—

We had, says the writer, calculated to come up with the brute where it had been seen half an hour before; but no sooner had one of our men, who was walking foremost, seen the animal at the distance of some fifteen or twenty fathoms, than he exclaimed, 'There! there!' and immediately took to his heels, and we all followed his example. The elephant did not see us until we had run some fifteen or twenty paces from the spot where we turned, when he gave us chase, screaming frightfully as he came on. The Englishman managed to climb a tree, and the rest of my companions did the same; as for myself, I could not, although I made one or two superhuman efforts. But there was no time to be lost. The elephant was running at me with his trunk bent down in a curve towards the ground. At this critical moment Mr. Lindsay held out his foot to me, with the help of which and then of the branches of the tree, which were three or four feet above my head, I managed to scramble up to a branch. The elephant came directly to the tree and attempted to force it down, which he could not. He first coiled his trunk round the stem, and pulled it with all his might, but with no effect. He then applied his head to the tree, and pushed for several minutes, but with no better success. He then trampled with his feet all the projecting roots, moving, as he did so, several times round and round the tree. Lastly, failing in all this, and seeing a pile of timber, which I had lately cut, at a short distance from us, he removed it all (thirty-six pieces) one at a time to the root of the tree, and piled them up in a regular business-like manner; then placing his hind feet on this pile, he raised the fore part of his body, and reached out his trunk, but still he could not touch us, as we were too far above him. The Englishman then fired, and the ball took effect somewhere on the elephant's head, but did not kill him. It made him only the more furious. The next shot, however, levelled him to the ground. I afterwards brought the skull of the animal to Colombo, and it is still to be seen at the house of Mr. Armitage.

Another highly curious trait in the emotional psychology of the elephant is the readiness with which the huge animal expires under the mere influence of what the natives call a 'broken heart.' The facts on this head are without a parallel in any other animal, and are the more remarkable from the fact that, so far as natural length of life is any token, the elephant may be said to have more vitality, or innate power of living, than any other terrestrial mammal. Again, to quote from Sir E. Tennent:—

Amongst the last of the elephants noosed was the *rogue*. Though far more savage than the others, he joined in none of their charges and assaults on the fences, as they uniformly drove him off, and would not permit him to enter their circle. When dragged past another of his companions in misfortune, who was lying exhausted on the ground, he flew upon him and attempted to fasten his teeth in his head; this was the only instance of viciousness which occurred during the progress of the corral. When tied up and overpowered, he was at first noisy and violent, but soon lay down peacefully, a sign, according to the hunters, that his death was at hand. Their prognostication was correct; he continued for about twelve hours to cover himself with dust like the others, and to moisten it with water from his trunk; but at length he lay exhausted, and died so calmly, that having been moving but a few moments before, his death was only perceived by the myriads of black flies by which his body was almost instantly covered, although not one was visible a moment before.

But this peculiarity is not confined to rogue elephants. Thus Captain Yule, in his 'Narrative of an Embassy to Ava in 1855,' records an illustration of this tendency of the elephant to sudden death. One newly captured, the process of taming which was exhibited to the British Envoy, 'made vigorous resistance to the placing of a collar on its neck, and the people were proceeding to tighten it, when the elephant, which had lain down as if quite exhausted, reared suddenly on the hind quarters, and fell on its side—*dead*!'

Mr. Strachan noticed the same liability of the elephants to sudden death from very slight causes. 'Of the fall,' he says, 'at any time, though on plain ground, they either die immediately, or languish till they die; their great weight occasioning them so much hurt by the fall.'

And Sir E. Tennent observes that,—
In the process of taming, the presence of the tame ones can generally be dispensed with after two months, and the captive may then be ridden by the driver alone; and after three or four months he may be entrusted with

labour, so far as regards docility; but it is undesirable, and even involves the risk of life, to work an elephant too soon; it has frequently happened that a valuable animal has lain down and died the first time it was tried in harness, from what the natives believed to be 'broken heart,' certainly without any cause inferable from injury or previous disease.

Nor is this tendency to die under the influence of mere emotion restricted to the effect of a 'broken heart;' it seems also to occur under the power of strong emotional disturbances of other kinds. For instance, an elephant caught and trained by Mr. Cripps is thus alluded to by Sir E. Tennent:—

This was the largest elephant that had been tamed in Ceylon; he measured upwards of nine feet at the shoulders, and belonged to the caste so highly prized for the temples. He was gentle after his first capture, but his removal from the corral to the stables, though only a distance of six miles, was a matter of the extremest difficulty; his extraordinary strength rendering him more than a match for the attendant decoys. He on one occasion escaped, but was recaptured in the forest; and he afterwards became so docile as to perform a variety of tricks. He was at length ordered to be removed to Colombo; but such was his terror on approaching the fort, that on coaxing him to enter the gate he became paralysed in the extraordinary way elsewhere alluded to, and *died on the spot.*

General Intelligence.

The higher mental faculties of the elephant are more advanced in their development than in any other animal, except the dog and monkey. I shall, therefore, devote some considerable space to the narration of instances of its display. The general fact that elephants are habitually employed in certain parts of India for the purposes of building, storing timber, &c., in itself shows a level of docile intelligence which only that of the dog can rival; but I shall here confine myself to stating special instances of the display of sagacity unusually high, even for the elephant.

Captain Shipp, in his 'Memoirs,' gives the following incident, of which he was an eye-witness. During a march with guns in the mountainous districts of India, the force of which he was a member came to a steep ascent. A staircase of logs was prepared to enable the elephants to ascend the slope. When all was ready the first elephant was led to the bottom of the staircase:—

He looked up, shook his head, and when forced by his driver, roared piteously. There can be no question, in my opinion, but that this sagacious animal was competent instinctively to judge of the practicability of the artificial flight of steps thus constructed; for the moment some little alteration had been made, he seemed willing to approach. He then commenced his examination and scrutiny by pressing with his trunk the trees that had been thrown across; and after this he put his fore-leg on with great caution... The next step for him to ascend by was a projecting rock, which he could not remove. Here the same sagacious examination took place, the elephant keeping his flat side close to the side of the trunk, and leaning against it. The next step was against a tree, but this, on the first pressure of his trunk, he did not like. Here the driver made use of the most endearing epithets, such as 'Wonderful,' 'My life,' 'Well done, my dear,' 'My dove,' 'My son,' 'My wife;' but all these endearing appellations, of which elephants are so fond, would not induce him to try again. Force was at length resorted to, and the elephant roared terrifically, but would not move.

Something was then altered, the elephant was satisfied, and at last succeeded in mounting to the top of the staircase:—
On reaching the top his delight was visible in a most eminent degree; he caressed his keepers, and threw dirt about in a most playful manner. Another elephant, a much younger animal, had now to follow. He had watched the ascent of the other with the utmost interest, making motions all the while as though he was assisting him by

shouldering him up the acclivity, in such gestures as I have seen some men make when spectators of gymnastic exercises. When he saw his comrade up, he evinced his pleasure by giving a salute something like the sound of a trumpet. When called upon to take his turn, however, he seemed much alarmed, and would not act at all without force.

After a performance similar to that of the previous elephant, however, he too neared the top, when 'the other, who had already performed his task, extended his trunk to the assistance of his brother in distress, round which the younger animal entwined his, and thus reached the summit.' There was then a cordial greeting between the two animals, 'as if they had been long separated from each other, and had just escaped from some perilous achievement. They mutually embraced each other, and stood face to face for a considerable time, as if whispering congratulations.'

Mr. Jesse says: 'I was one day feeding the poor elephant (who was so barbarously put to death at Exeter Change) with potatoes, which he took out of my hand. One of them, a round one, fell on the floor, just out of reach of his proboscis.' After several ineffectual attempts to reach it, 'he at length *blew* the potato against the opposite wall with sufficient force to make it rebound, and he then without difficulty secured it.'

This remarkable observation has fortunately been corroborated by Mr. Darwin. He writes:—

I have seen, as I dare say have others, that when a small object is thrown on the ground beyond the reach of one of the elephants at the Zoological Gardens, he blows through his trunk on the ground beyond the object, so that the current reflected on all sides may drive the object within his reach.

The observation has also been corroborated by other observers.

The following is quoted from Mr. Watson's book:—

Of the elephant's sense and judgment the following instance is given as a well-known fact in a letter of Dr. Daniel Wilson, Bishop of Calcutta, to his son in England, printed in a Life of the bishop, published a few years ago. An elephant belonging to an Engineer officer in his diocese had a disease in his eyes, and had for three days been completely blind. His owner asked Dr. Webb, a physician intimate with the bishop, if he could do anything for the relief of the animal. Dr. Webb replied that he was willing to try, on one of the eyes, the effect of nitrate of silver, which was a remedy commonly used for similar diseases in the human eye.

The animal was accordingly made to lie down, and when the nitrate of silver was applied, uttered a terrific roar at the acute pain which it occasioned. But the effect of the application was wonderful, for the eye was in a great degree restored, and the elephant could partially see. The doctor was in consequence ready to operate similarly on the other eye on the following day; and the animal, when he was brought out and heard the doctor's voice, lay down of himself, placed his head quietly on one side, curled up his trunk, drew in his breath like a human being about to endure a painful operation, gave a sigh of relief when it was over, and then, by motions of his trunk and other gestures, gave evident signs of wishing to express his gratitude. Here we plainly see in the elephant memory, understanding, and reasoning from one thing to another. The animal remembered the benefit that he had felt from the application to one eye, and when he was brought to the same place on the following day and heard the operator's voice, he concluded that a like service was to be done to his other eye.

The fact that elephants exhibit this sagacious fortitude under surgical operations—thus resembling, as we shall afterwards observe, both dogs and monkeys—is corroborated by another instance given in Bingley's 'Animal Biography,' and serves to render credible the following story given in the same work:—
In the last war in India a young elephant received a violent wound in its head, the pain of which rendered it so frantic and ungovernable that it was found impossible to persuade the animal to have the part dressed. Whenever anyone approached it ran off with fury, and would suffer no person to come within several yards of it. The man who had

care of it at length hit upon a contrivance for securing it. By a few words and signs he gave the mother of the animal sufficient intelligence of what was wanted; the sensible creature immediately seized her young one with her trunk, and held it firmly down, though groaning with agony, while the surgeon completely dressed the wound; and she continued to perform this service every day till the animal was perfectly recovered.

Again, as still further corroboration of this point, I may quote the following from Sir E. Tennent's 'Natural History of Ceylon:'— Nothing can more strongly exhibit the impulse to obedience in the elephant than the patience with which, at the order of his keeper, he swallows the nauseous medicines of the native elephant-doctors; and it is impossible to witness the fortitude with which (without shrinking) he submits to excruciating surgical operations for the removal of tumours and ulcers to which he is subject, without conceiving a vivid impression of his gentleness and intelligence. Dr. Davy when in Ceylon was consulted about an elephant in the Government stud, which was suffering from a deep, burrowing sore in the back, just over the back-bone, which had long resisted the treatment ordinarily employed. He recommended the use of the knife, that issue might be given to the accumulated matter, but no one of the attendants was competent to undertake the operation. 'Being assured,' he continues, 'that the creature would behave well, I undertook it myself. The elephant was not bound, but was made to kneel down at his keeper's command; and with an amputating knife, using all my force, I made the incision required through the tough integuments. The elephant did not flinch, but rather inclined towards me when using the knife; and merely uttered a low, and as it were suppressed groan. In short, he behaved as like a human being as possible, as if conscious (as I believe he was) that the operation was for his good, and the pain unavoidable.'

Major Skinner witnessed the following display of intelligent action by a large herd of wild elephants. During the hot season at Nenera Kalama the elephants have a difficulty in finding water, and are therefore obliged to congregate in large numbers where water is to be obtained. Being stationed near a water supply, and knowing that a large herd of elephants were in the neighbourhood, Major Skinner resolved to watch their proceedings. On a moonlight night, therefore, he climbed a tree about four hundred yards from the water, and waited patiently for two hours before he heard or saw anything of the elephants. At length he saw a huge beast issue from the wood, and advance cautiously across the open ground to within a hundred yards of the tank, where he stood perfectly motionless; and the rest of the herd, meanwhile, were so quiet that not the least sound was to be heard from them. Gradually, at three successive advances, halting some minutes after each, he moved up to the water's edge, in which, however, he did not think proper to quench his thirst, but remained for several minutes listening in perfect stillness. He then returned cautiously and slowly to the point at which he had issued from the wood, from whence he came back with five other elephants, with which he proceeded, somewhat less slowly than before, to within a few yards of the tank, where he posted them as patrols. He then re-entered the wood and collected the whole herd, which must have amounted to between eighty and a hundred, and led them across

the open ground with the most extraordinary
composure and quiet till they came up to the
five sentinels, when he left them for a
moment, and again made a reconnaissance at
the edge of the tank. At last, being
apparently satisfied that all was safe, he
turned back, and obviously gave the order to
advance; 'for in a moment,' says Major
Skinner, 'the whole herd rushed to the water
with a degree of unreserved confidence so
opposite to the caution and timidity which
had marked their previous movements, that
nothing will ever persuade me that there was
not rational and preconcerted cooperation
throughout the whole party, and a degree of
responsible authority exercised by the
patriarch-leader.'

Mr. H. L. Jenkins writes to me:—
What I particularly wish to observe is that
there are good reasons for supposing that

elephants possess abstract ideas; for instance, I think it is impossible to doubt that they acquire through their own experience notions of hardness and weight, and the grounds on which I am led to think this are as follows. A captured elephant after he has been taught his ordinary duty, say about three months after he is taken, is taught to pick up things from the ground and give them to his mahout sitting on his shoulders. Now for the first few months it is dangerous to require him to pick up anything but soft articles, such as clothes, because the things are often handed up with considerable force. After a time, longer with some elephants than others, they appear to take in a knowledge of the nature of the things they are required to lift, and the bundle of clothes will be thrown up sharply as before, but heavy things, such as a crowbar or piece of iron chain, will be handed up in a gentle manner; a sharp knife will be picked up by its handle and placed on the elephant's head, so that the mahout can also take it by the handle. I have purposely given elephants things to lift which they could never have seen before, and they were all handled in such a manner as to convince me that they recognised such qualities as hardness, sharpness, and weight. You are quite at liberty to make any use of these remarks you please if they are of service.

Again, as Dr. Lindley Kemp observes, 'the manner in which tame elephants assist in capturing wild ones affords us an instance of reasoning in an animal,' &c.; and similarly, Mr. Darwin observes: 'It is, I think, impossible to read the account given by Sir E. Tennent of the behaviour of the female elephants used as decoys, without admitting that they intentionally practise deceit.'

The following is an extract from the more interesting of the observations to which Mr.

Darwin here alludes, and I think it is impossible to read them without assenting to his judgment. Several herds of wild elephants having been driven into a corral, two tame decoys were ridden into it:—

One was of prodigious age, having been in the service of the Dutch and English Governments in succession for upwards of a century. The other, called by her keeper 'Siribeddi,' was about fifty years old, and distinguished for gentleness and docility. She was a most accomplished decoy, and evinced the utmost relish for the sport. Having entered the corral noiselessly, carrying a mahout on her shoulders with the headman of the noosers seated behind him, she moved slowly along with a sly composure and an assumed air of easy indifference; sauntering leisurely in the direction of the captives, and halting now and then to pluck a bunch of grass or a few leaves as she passed. As she approached the herd they put themselves in motion to meet her, and the leader, having advanced in front and passed his trunk gently over her head, turned and paced slowly back to his dejected companions. Siribeddi followed with the same listless step, and drew herself up close behind him, thus affording the nooser an opportunity to stoop under her and slip the noose over the hind foot of the wild one. The latter instantly perceived his danger, shook off the rope, and turned to attack the man. He would have suffered for his temerity had not Siribeddi protected him by raising her trunk and driving the assailant into the midst of the herd, when the old man, being slightly wounded, was helped out of the corral, and his son, Ranghanie, took his place.

The herd again collected in a circle, with their heads towards the centre. The largest male was singled out, and two tame ones pushed boldly in, one on either side of him, till the three stood nearly abreast. He made no resistance, but betrayed his uneasiness by shifting restlessly from foot to foot. Ranghanie now crept up, and holding the rope open with both hands (its other extremity being made fast to Siribeddi's collar), and watching the instant when the wild elephant lifted its hind foot, succeeded in passing the noose over its leg, drew it close, and fled to the rear. The two tame elephants instantly fell back, Siribeddi stretched the rope to its full length, and whilst she dragged out the captive, her companion placed himself between her and the herd to prevent any interference.

In order to tie him to a tree he had to be drawn backwards some twenty or thirty yards, making furious resistance, bellowing in terror, plunging on all sides, and crushing the smaller timber, which bent like reeds beneath his clumsy struggles. Siribeddi drew him steadily after her, and wound the rope round the proper tree, holding it all the time at its full tension, and stepping cautiously across it when, in order to give it a second turn, it was necessary to pass between the tree and the elephant. With a coil round the stem, however, it was beyond her strength to haul the prisoner close up, which was, nevertheless, necessary in order to make him perfectly fast; but the second tame one, perceiving the difficulty, returned from the herd, confronted the struggling prisoner, pushed him shoulder to shoulder, and head to head, forcing him backwards, whilst at every step Siribeddi hauled in the slackened rope till she brought him fairly up to the foot of the tree, where he was made fast by the cooroowe people. A second noose was then passed over the other hind-leg, and secured like the first, both legs being afterwards hobbled together by ropes made from the fibre of the kitool or jaggery palm, which, being more flexible than that of the cocoa-nut, occasions less formidable ulcerations. The two decoys then ranged themselves, as before, abreast of the prisoner on either side, thus enabling Ranghanie to stoop under them and noose the two fore-feet as he had already done the hind; and these ropes being made fast to the tree in front, the capture was complete, and the tame elephants and keepers withdrew to repeat the operation on another of the herd.

The second victim singled out from the herd was secured in the same manner as the first. It was a female. The tame ones forced themselves in on either side as before, cutting her off from her companions, whilst Ranghanie stooped under them and attached the fatal noose, and Siribeddi dragged her out amidst unavailing struggles, when she was made fast by each leg to the nearest group of strong trees. When the noose was placed upon her fore-foot, she seized it with her trunk, and succeeded in carrying it to her mouth, where she would speedily have severed it had not a tame elephant interfered, and placing his foot on the rope pressed it downwards out of her jaws..... The conduct of the tame ones during all these proceedings was truly wonderful. They displayed the most perfect conception of every movement, both of the object to be attained and of the means to accomplish it. They manifested the utmost enjoyment in what was going on. There was no ill-humour, no malignity in the spirit displayed, in what was otherwise a heartless proceeding, but they set about it in a way that showed a thorough relish for it, as an agreeable pastime. Their caution was as remarkable as their sagacity; there was no hurrying, no confusion, they never ran foul of the ropes, were never in the way of the animals already noosed; and amidst the most violent struggles, when the tame ones had frequently to step across the captives, they in no instance trampled on them, or occasioned the slightest accident or annoyance. So far from this, they saw intuitively a difficulty or a danger, and addressed themselves unbidden to remove it. In tying up one of the larger elephants, he contrived, before he could be hauled close up to the tree, to walk once or twice round it, carrying the rope with him; the decoy, perceiving the advantage he had thus gained over the nooser, walked up of her own accord, and pushed him backwards with her head, till she made him unwind himself again; upon which the rope was hauled tight and made fast. More than once, when a wild one was extending his trunk, and would have intercepted the rope about to be placed over his leg, Siribeddi, by a sudden motion of her own trunk, pushed his aside, and prevented him; and on one occasion, when successive efforts had failed to put the noose over the fore-leg of an elephant which was already secured by one foot, but which wisely put the other to the ground as often as it was attempted to pass the noose under it, I saw the decoy watch her opportunity, and when his foot was again raised, suddenly push in her own leg beneath it, and hold it up till the noose was attached and drawn tight.

One could almost fancy there was a display of dry humour in the manner in which the decoys thus played with the fears of the wild herd, and made light of their efforts at resistance. When reluctant they shoved them forward, when violent they drove them back; when the wild ones threw themselves down, the tame ones butted them with head and shoulders, and forced them up again. And when it was necessary to keep them down, they knelt upon them, and prevented them from rising, till the ropes were secured.

At every moment of leisure they fanned themselves with a bunch of leaves, and the graceful ease with which an elephant uses his trunk on such occasions is very striking. It is doubtless owing to the combination of a circular with a horizontal movement in that flexible limb; but it is impossible to see an elephant fanning himself without being struck by the singular elegance of motion which he displays. The tame ones, too, indulged in the luxury of dusting themselves with sand, by flinging it from their trunks; but it was a curious illustration of their delicate sagacity, that so long as the mahout was on their necks, they confined themselves to flinging the dust along their sides and stomach, as if aware that to throw it over their heads and back would cause annoyance to their riders.

Sir E. Tennent has also some observations on other uses to which tame elephants are put, which are well worth quoting. Thus, speaking of the labour of piling timber, he says that the elephant manifests an intelligence and dexterity which are surprising to a stranger, because the sameness of the operation enables the animal to go on for hours disposing of log after log, almost without a hint or direction from his attendant. For example, two elephants employed in piling ebony and satinwood in the yards attached to the commissariat stores at Colombo, were so accustomed to their work, that they were able to accomplish it with equal precision and with greater rapidity than if it had been done by dock-labourers. When the pile attained a certain height, and they were no longer able by their conjoint efforts to raise one of the heavy logs of ebony to the summit, they had been taught to lean two pieces against the heap, up the inclined plane of which they gently rolled the remaining logs, and placed them trimly on the top.

It has been asserted that in their occupations 'elephants are to a surprising extent the creatures of habit,' that their movements are altogether mechanical, and that 'they are annoyed by any deviation from their accustomed practice, and resent any constrained departure from the regularity of their course.' So far as my own observation goes, this is incorrect; and I am assured by officers of experience, that in regard to changing his treatment, his hours or his occupation, an elephant evinces no more consideration than a horse, but exhibits the same pliancy and facility.

At one point, however, the utility of the elephant stops short. Such is the intelligence and earnestness he displays in work, which he seems to conduct almost without supervision, that it has been assumed that he would continue his labour, and accomplish his given task, as well in the absence of his keeper as during his presence. But here his innate love of ease displays itself, and if the eye of his attendant be withdrawn, the moment he has finished the thing immediately in hand, he will stroll away lazily, to browse or enjoy the luxury of fanning himself and blowing dust over his back.

The means of punishing so powerful an animal is a question of difficulty to his attendants. Force being almost inapplicable, they try to work on his passions and feelings, by such expedients as altering the nature of his food or withholding it altogether for a time. On such occasions the demeanour of the creature will sometimes evince a sense of humiliation as well as of discontent. In some parts of India it is customary, in dealing with offenders, to stop their allowance of sugar canes or of jaggery; or to restrain them from eating their own share of fodder and leaves till their companions shall have finished; and in such cases the consciousness of degradation betrayed by the looks and attitudes of the culprit is quite sufficient to identify him, and to excite a feeling of sympathy and pity.

The elephant's obedience to his keeper is the result of affection, as well as of fear; and although his attachment becomes so strong that an elephant in Ceylon has been known to remain out all night, without food, rather than abandon his mahout, lying intoxicated in the jungle, yet he manifests little difficulty in yielding the same submission to a new driver in the event of a change of attendants.

Lastly, Sir E. Tennent writes:—
One evening, whilst riding in the vicinity of Candy, towards the scene of the massacre of Major Dabies' party in 1803, my horse evinced some excitement at a noise which approached us in the thick jungle, and which consisted of a repetition of the ejaculation *urmph! urmph!* in a hoarse and dissatisfied tone. A turn in the forest explained the mystery, by bringing us face to face with a tame elephant, unaccompanied by any attendant. He was labouring painfully to carry a heavy beam of timber, which he balanced across his tusks, but, the pathway being narrow, he was forced to bend his head to one side to permit it to pass endways; and the exertion and this inconvenience combined led him to utter the dissatisfied

sounds which disturbed the composure of my horse. On seeing us halt, the elephant raised his head, reconnoitred us for a moment, then flung down the timber, and voluntarily forced himself backwards among the brushwood so as to leave a passage, of which he expected us to avail ourselves. My horse hesitated: the elephant observed it, and impatiently thrust himself deeper into the jungle, repeating his cry of *urmph!* but in a voice evidently meant to encourage us to advance. Still the horse trembled; and, anxious to observe the instinct of the two sagacious animals, I forebore any interference: again the elephant of his own accord wedged himself further in amongst the trees, and manifested some impatience that we did not pass him. At length the horse moved forward; and when we were fairly past, I saw the wise creature stoop and take up its heavy burden, trim and balance it on its tusks, and resume its route as before, hoarsely snorting its discontented remonstrance.

Dr. Erasmus Darwin records an observation which was communicated to him by a 'gentleman of undoubted veracity,' of an elephant in India which the keeper was in the habit of leaving to play the part of nurse to his child when he and his wife had occasion to go away from home. The elephant was chained up, and whenever the child in its creeping about came to the end of the elephant's tether, he used gently to draw it back again with his trunk.

In *'Nature,'* vol. xix., Mr. J. J. Furniss writes:—
In Central Park one very hot day my attention was drawn to the conduct of an elephant which had been placed in an enclosure in the open air. On the ground was

a large heap of newly-mown grass, which the sagacious animal was taking up by the trunkful, and laying carefully upon his sun-heated back. He continued the operation until his back was *completely thatched*, when he remained quiet, apparently enjoying the result of his ingenuity.

Mr. Furniss in a later communication (vol. xx., p. 21) continues:—
Since the publication of my former letter (as above), I have received additional data bearing on the subject from Mr. W. A. Conklin, the superintendent of the Central Park Menagerie. I am informed by him that he has frequently observed elephants, when out of doors in the hot sunshine, thatch their backs with hay or grass; that they do so to a certain extent when under cover in the summer time, and when the flies which then attack the animals, often so fiercely as to

draw blood, are particularly numerous; but that they never attempt to thatch their backs in winter. This seems to prove that they act intelligently for the attainment of a definite end. It would be interesting to learn whether elephants in their wild state are in the habit of so thatching their backs. It seems more probable to suppose that in their native wilds they would avail themselves of the natural shade afforded by the jungle, and that the habit is one which has been developed in consequence of their changed surroundings in captivity.

Mr. G. E. Peal writes to 'Nature' (vol. xxi., p. 34):—
One evening, soon after my arrival in Eastern Assam, and while the five elephants were as usual being fed opposite the bungalow, I observed a young and lately caught one step up to a bamboo-stake fence,

and quietly pull one of the stakes up. Placing it under foot, it broke a piece off with the trunk, and after lifting it to its mouth threw it away. It repeated this twice or thrice, and then drew another stake and began again. Seeing that the bamboo was old and dry I asked the reason of this, and was told to wait and see what it would do. At last it seemed to get a piece that suited, and holding it in the trunk firmly, and stepping the left fore-leg well forward, passed the piece of bamboo under the armpit, so to speak, and began to scratch with some force. My surprise reached its climax when I saw a large elephant leech fall on the ground, quite six inches long and thick as one's finger, and which, from its position, could not easily be detached without this scraper or scratcher which was deliberately made by the elephant. I subsequently found that it was a common occurrence. Such scrapers are used by every elephant daily.

On another occasion, when travelling at a time of the year when the large flies are so tormenting to an elephant, I noticed that the one I rode had no fan or wisp to beat them off with. The mahout, at my order, slackened pace and allowed her to go to the side of the road, when for some moments she moved along rummaging the smaller jungle on the bank; at last she came to a cluster of young shoots well branched, and after feeling among them and selecting one, raised her trunk and neatly stripped down the stem, taking off all the lower branches and leaving a fine bunch on top. She deliberately cleaned it down several times, and then laying hold at the lower end broke off a beautiful fan or switch about five feet long, handle included. With this she kept the flies at bay as we went along, flapping them off on each side.

Say what we may, these are both really *bonâ fide* implements, each intelligently made for a definite purpose.

My friend Mrs. A. S. H. Richardson sends me the following. The Rev. Mr. Townsend, who narrated the episode, is personally known to her:—
An elephant was chained to a tree in the compound opposite Mr. Townsend's house. Its driver made an oven at a short distance, in which he put his rice-cakes to bake, and then covered them with stones and grass and went away. When he was gone, the elephant with his trunk unfastened the chain round his foot, went to the oven and uncovered it, took out and ate the cakes, re-covered the oven with the stones and grass as before, and went back to his place. He could not fasten the chain again round his own foot, so he twisted it round and round it, in order to look the same,

and when the driver returned the elephant was standing with his back to the oven. The driver went to his cakes, discovered the theft, and, looking round, caught the elephant's eye as he looked back over his shoulder out of the corner of it. Instantly he detected the culprit, and condign punishment followed. The whole occurrence was witnessed from the windows by the family.

Chapter 2[2]

I.

On the Intelligence of the Elephants.

In determining the intelligence of an animal, we naturally take ourselves as the type of mental excellence, and grade the lower animals as they approach us. Some would place the ant next to man, arguing that it more closely resembles him in its habits, customs, and methods of showing what we consider the result of intelligent action. It keeps domestic animals (*aphis*), goes to war in organized bodies, makes slaves of other insects, erects wonderful structures, is accredited with planting seeds, and certainly stores them up after arranging them so that they cannot sprout; in fact, appears to act in

---

[2] C. F. Holder, in *The Ivory King: A popular history of the elephant and its allies.*

many ways like a rational human being: and, contrasted to it, the elephant, dog, horse, and beaver would seem to be comparatively stupid animals; at least, such would be the verdict of the observer who mistakes instinct for reason. Such a comparison seems unfair to the other animals mentioned; and to argue that the elephant is not as intelligent as the ant because it does not build a house, and lay up a food-supply, would hardly be just, as the great proboscidian does not require such shelter: and, without instancing any more examples, it would appear, that, to establish the relative intelligence of an animal, it should be judged, not especially by the standard of another, but according to its displayal of what we term thought; and this leads us to consider how thought may be exhibited in an animal. Instinctive action is something that is done without appreciable thought: thus, a colt instinctively kicks at an enemy, as a kitten spits at a dog.

The fear of this animal has been present in all the generations of cats, and is inherited, as shown by the protest in the curve of the back, the raising of the tail, and other familiar methods of expression. So we may, without multiplying instances, consider that instinctive action is the outward expression of inherited experience, and has practically nothing in common with that action of the mind which we call thought. If this kitten when it grows older,—and I know of an instance,—should without instruction climb upon a door, and lift the latch, she would be exhibiting a practical illustration of the results of thought: in other words, she would lift the latch because she knew that the door could not be opened without it, and consequently had, in her feline mind, turned over to some extent the relations that existed between the latch, the door, and the object she had in view. So if the colt should go to a pump, as a cow is alleged to have done, and take the handle in its mouth without being taught, and pump water to drink, it would show that the animal had used its powers of thought. Now, what position does the elephant take in the scale of intelligence?

The Hindoos of the present day do not consider the elephant a remarkably intelligent animal. Yet at one time its sagacity was certainly appreciated, as the Hindoo god of wisdom is figured with the body of a man and the head of an elephant; and A. W. Schlegel states that in very early times they marvelled at everything about the animal, especially its sagacity, which made it seem to them the embodiment of the god Ganessa.

Probably Dr. Dalton expresses the latest knowledge touching this subject. He says,—

"If we examine the comparative development of the hemispheres of the brain in different species of animals, and in different races of men, we shall find that the size of these ganglia corresponds very closely with the degree of intelligence possessed by the individual.... Among quadrupeds, the elephant has much the largest, and most perfectly formed, cerebrum, in proportion to the size of the entire body; and, of all quadrupeds, he is proverbially the most intelligent and the most teachable.

It is important to observe, in this connection, that the kind of intelligence which characterizes the elephant and some other of the lower animals, and which most nearly resembles that of man, is a *teachable* intelligence,—a very different thing from the intelligence which depends upon instinct, such as that of insects, for example, or birds of passage."

In a previous work I mentioned that Mr. H. H. Cross informed me that he had seen an elephant of the Barnum herd select a stick, and probe the small orifice in the temple. Since then I have seen a statement by Mr. Cross in print, to the effect that he has seen the elephant select a twig, examine it carefully with one of its keen little eyes, by holding it up in its trunk, and, if it found it was not sharp enough for the purpose, deliberately grind down the point by rubbing it upon a stone, and, when its shape suited him, use it to open the orifice.

In Africa, according to Drummond, the wild elephants migrate south in time for certain fruits, which shows that they must remember the pleasures of the past season.

The migration is not suggested by a lack of food, as the supply of mimosa and other trees does not give out. When a wild elephant takes a branch in its trunk, and uses it to brush away flies, it shows more intelligence than it is generally given credit for; while its lodging dust and sand on its back to prevent the attack of these pests, is also to be considered an intelligent act. Elephants are extremely cautious, and this has been used as an argument against their intelligence. Sanderson says that the animal is stupid because the simplest fence is often sufficient to protect grain from them; but I am inclined to think that this is owing to their extreme caution: the fence may have in their mind some association with the pitfall, or traps of some kind, which have been met in their experience.

An elephant will rarely step upon a bridge that is not safe, and many instances could be cited showing that their protests and objections were founded upon an intelligent appreciation of danger. Sanderson says also that the elephant lacks originality: but the two instances I have mentioned,—namely, using a branch to brush off flies, and sharpening the stick,—will, I think, in the opinion of my young readers, free the great animal from this imputation; and I do not recall many actions performed by *wild* animals, that show more appreciation of the practical application of cause and effect.

The intelligence of the elephant has been a subject of varied appreciation. Many observers have considered remarkable actions of elephants involuntary, when in truth they were merely obeying the commands of their riders or mahouts, who expressed their wishes by the pressure of their legs, or by the voice, which was not seen or heard by the observer. When

Tavernier was travelling with the Mahommedan army of the Mogul, he was astonished to see the elephants seize the little images which stood before the pagodas, and dash them to the ground. The Hindoos readily believed that the elephant did this from a religious aversion to the idols, but the traveller knew that the mahouts were secretly directing the great animals. So, in passing in review before the king, the elephants did not salute until coming to his majesty.

Once when two elephants were at a spring, the largest violently seized a bucket carried by the smaller, and began to dip up water; upon which the other elephant drew back, and butted its companion so that it fell headlong into the pool. This story is told to illustrate the revengeful nature of the animal, when, in point of fact, the entire action was instigated by the mahout upon its back. The most remarkable trait of the elephant is its obedience: and if we were to take its aptitude to learn the tasks described in the chapter on trained elephants, as a test of intelligence, it would certainly hold its own among all animals; as, considering that it is perhaps the most ungainly, and certainly the heaviest, of all land animals, its various feats are indeed remarkable.

At the slightest pressure of its rider's foot it will salute, lift the trunk in the air, and trumpet loudly; stop, back, lie down to enable the mahout to dismount, roll over, lift the man upon its trunk, pass over his body with the greatest ease, lift stones from the ground for the driver to throw at other elephants, and even tie itself up at night; in fact, among all trained animals, dogs, horses, or birds, none compare with the elephant in their obedience, and intelligent appreciation of what is required. Though "playing 'possum" or feigning death can hardly be cited as an evidence of intelligence, it may be interesting to know that it is sometimes attempted by elephants. Sir Emerson Tennent was informed by Mr. Cripps that he was aware of an instance where an elephant adopted this ruse to secure its freedom. It had been led into a corral between two tame elephants, and upon being released sank to the ground apparently lifeless. Every attempt to revive it, or force it to show any evidence of life, failed; and the natives believed that it had died of a broken heart,—a term that they often apply when an elephant dies without apparent cause. Finally the body was abandoned as lifeless; and, as soon as the hunters had gone a short distance, the wily brute regained its feet, and rushed for the jungle, screaming at the top of its voice; its cries of evident delight being heard long after it had disappeared. In the various chapters of this work, other instances have been cited showing that, far from being a stupid animal, the elephant in its *wild* state exhibits far more intelligence than the wild dog or horse; and when we compare the animals after their so-called education, there is little that the trained dog can do that is not accomplished by the elephant; and while it is difficult to draw exact lines, and point out the exact mental status of the elephant in the rank and file of the lower animals, I would place it well to the front among mammals.

I am glad to be able to bring to the support of my belief in the superior intelligence of the elephant, the testimony of a naturalist and careful observer, Col. Nicholas Pike, late consul at Mauritius, whose extensive travels and long residence in the East render his opinions of especial value and interest. The following is Col. Pike's letter in answer to my request for an expression of his opinion upon the subject:—

Mr. C. F. Holder.

My dear Sir,—In answer to your questions as to my opinion relative to the intelligence of the elephant, I will jot down a few notes that may interest you.

This animal is to my mind one of the most intelligent of the brute creation. I am led to this conclusion from what I have actually seen, and from reliable information given me by persons who have devoted a lifetime to studying their habits and life-history generally. I think that in elephants, as in other animals,—and we see even in man himself,—there is a great difference in the amount of intelligence they possess.

A friend of mine, who owned many of these animals, placed an old tame male that appeared sick, in a pasture, where he had also some horses and sheep feeding, thinking it would recuperate "Dick," who was a great favorite. The whole pasture was well fenced in, and the gate was securely bolted. One morning when I was visiting my friend, we were surprised to see "Dick" let himself in by the back-gate; and he warned us of his presence by trumpeting. His master went to him, and asked what he wanted. The beast at once took up a pitcher containing water which was nearby, and poured some of it on the ground, attempting to sip a few drops of it with his trunk. His master, seeing what he wanted, gave him water, and told him to go back. Thinking the gate must have been left open, and perhaps the sheep and horses straying out, we followed, but to our surprise found the gate shut, and not only bolted, but the bolt turned up in the little slot so that it should not be easily opened. We waited, curious to see what Dick would do. As soon as he reached the gate, he deliberately moved the bolt, and passed into the field, then turning round, he re-adjusted the bolt as well as I could have done it, and marched off contentedly to a favorite corner under some trees.

I have seen my friend quietly call individuals by their name out of the herd; and in one instance, a female, "Maggie," was called, and told to take me on her back, which she did, helping me up carefully with her trunk. I have seen an elephant draw a cork from a bottle of claret, and drink the contents without spilling a drop. I saw four or five called singly by name from their grazing-ground, form in line, and bow, and kneel before a group of ladies, and then march back in as regular order at the word of command as a file of soldiers.

Hundreds of elephants are employed in the government service in the three presidencies of India,—Calcutta, Bombay and Madras. They go through a regular routine, and know their hours for work and recreation as well as the man who watches the clock. When the bell sounds in the morning, they take up their line of march, to the lumber-yards for instance, where vast piles of beams and planks are stored. As soon as they arrive, each takes up his work, left from the day before. Great logs and beams are rolled along by the aid of the trunk, and, when near the pile, are lifted, two elephants to each beam, and hoisted into place, when they walk round and adjust their work with as much precision as a man would use with a plumb-line. When the usual hour for quitting work arrives, nothing can induce the creatures to go on; and you can't fool them on the time either, by ringing the bell late. Off they go to get their afternoon bath, where they will lie and wallow in the muddy water for hours. Their varied works require *cute* intelligence, not mere instinct, any more than you can attribute the good paving of a roadway by a poor laborer, who knows his business, though he may not be able to read or write, to instinct.

A circumstance was related to me by my friend, Gen. E. W. de Lansing Lowe, who was all through the campaign in India during the Sepoy rebellion. He said he had a very intelligent elephant that he constantly rode on, and as it was so hot they mostly travelled morning and evening. During the war, they came about the dusk of evening to a small bridge that spanned a deep ravine with water at the bottom. As soon as the elephant came to this bridge, no inducement could make him cross it. After some delay, finding all persuasion useless, the general determined to examine the structure. They found the enemy had cut away the supports of the bridge; and, had the elephant stepped on to it, the whole party would have been precipitated into the gulf below.

We have a notable instance of the sagacity of these animals at the time Barnum's circus was in Bridgeport a few years ago. A fire broke out in some sheds adjoining the tents, and it was feared the stables would catch the flames. They began to pull down the sheds, when someone suggested to bring out two elephants. This was done, and the animals set to with a will to pull down the place. They evidently at once took in the situation. They not only tore down the place, but threw the timbers so that they should not touch the tents, and beat out the flames. Now, if this does not show almost human reason, what does? They were put to the work on the spur of the moment, and not only performed it as if used to it, but actually did it more intelligently than many men would have done in such perilous circumstances. Had they not done so, as water was short, the loss of life to man and beast, and of property, might have been enormous.

If you could only interview Barnum, he could tell you more of the intelligence of the elephant than any man living.

I could relate numerous other incidents I have seen and been informed of; but enough has been said, I think, to prove how highly I think of the intelligence, sagacity, or whatever other name you may give it, of this unwieldly pachyderm.

II.

Elephants and their Friends.

All animals have their favorites or friends,—it may be some attendant or some animal to which they have formed an attachment,—and the elephant is no exception to the rule. Most of the latter's friends are made in confinement; but the wild animal has a number of little companions, which are of great value, at least, in adding to its comfort. These are birds; and chief among them is a beautiful crane, which is often seen—and, indeed, numbers of them—perched upon the back of the great animal, and riding about, presenting a strange and decided contrast to the dark-skinned proboscidian. The presence of these shy birds moving about on so curious a roost would seem a mystery; but, should we watch them, we should see that they were performing a most friendly act. They walk over the great, wrinkled back, and with their sharp eyes spy out all the insects which infest the great pachyderm, picking them out, and so securing a dinner and serving their friend at the same time, who probably is often driven to desperation by the myriads of insect-torments which abound in the dark continent. Besides the cranes, there are several smaller birds which are equally friendly to the king of beasts, and often congregate upon its back in great numbers; running about without fear, clinging to the huge ears, now dangling by the tail, and performing a still more friendly act at times in warning their friend of danger by rising in a flock, and uttering shrill cries, which arouse the drowsy elephant to a sense of its danger.

In confinement particularly, the elephant is famous for its friendships, attaching itself to certain persons or animals, showing its affection for them in various ways. One of the Barnum elephants formed a strong friendship for a large dog, which was fully reciprocated; the dog sleeping with its great friend, and always remaining about its feet. If it strayed away at any time, the elephant would look after it, and on its return show its delight and pleasure in many ways.

Elephants often become attached to children, and seem to display the greatest solicitude for them. They have been employed as nurses to extremely small children, performing the duties as care-taker with perfect satisfaction.

Though, as a rule, elephants obey their keepers from fear, there are cases where a decided friendship exists; and even when furious with rage, an elephant will often obey its keeper's voice. An affecting instance of this was seen in the case of the famous elephant Chuni, who was believed to have gone mad. The animal was taken out to be shot; and its keeper was obliged to order it to kneel, that the soldiers might shoot it. The man reluctantly gave the order; and the elephant obeyed the command, and fell, pierced by many bullets.

A mad elephant in Germany, which had destroyed much property, yielded immediately to the voice of the man who owned it, or had been its friend and keeper. The works of the ancient writers abound in instances of attachment and friendship between the huge animals and human beings. Ælian relates a story of an elephant who became passionately attached to a little girl who sold flowers in the streets of Antioch, and had occasionally given it a part of her store. Athenæus tells of one which became so fond of a little child, that it would eat only in its presence; but I fear that this story will not stand the test. Strabo states that elephants were known to have pined away and died when deprived of their keepers to whom they were attached. Lieut. Shipp gives, in his memoirs, a very minute account of an elephant, who, upon killing its keeper, was seized with what was considered a fit of remorse, which ultimately killed the animal. In other words, it died of "a broken heart," a term that is applied to-day to elephants in India who die of no apparent cause.

In Purchas's collection of travels, there is an account of an elephant who mourned for its master, the King of Ava, who was slain in battle, for many days; and, as the same is known to have occurred among dogs and cats at the present day, it is not at all improbable.

That the elephant should become attached to its keeper, is not strange. It is perfectly familiar with all his movements, receives all its food from him, is caressed and petted; and it is not surprising that at times the animals rebel when provided with an utter stranger to replace the one in whom they have learned to trust.

www.ingramcontent.com/pod-product-compliance
Lightning Source LLC
LaVergne TN
LVHW091727190726
843493LV00001B/487